Programming
Learn The Fundamentals Of Computer Programming Languages

By: Marc Rawen

2

has been made to provide accurate, up to date and reliable complete information. No warranties of any kind are expressed or implied. Readers acknowledge that the author is not engaging in the rendering of legal, financial, medical or professional advice.

By reading this document, the reader agrees that under no circumstances are we responsible for any losses, direct or indirect, which are incurred as a result of the use of information contained within this document, including, but not limited to, — errors, omissions, or inaccuracies.

Table of Contents

Introduction

Since you have bought this book, I must say, 'Welcome to the wonderful world of programming!' You see, programming is not just an activity but an entire world on its and by learning a language, you will be taking your first steps into this brave new world. After all, computers and computing technologies are everywhere, and a programming language is a foundation on which all of them are made possible.

Now, you may be interested in learning a programming language for a career in one of the many tech careers or simply as a hobby. Whatever be your reason, the fact is that you need to choose the right programming language to start with. You should learn some of the easiest programming languages to build up a strong base before proceeding further.

As such, this book deals with some of the best programming languages that a beginner should learn first before moving on to the harder ones. In this book, you will be learning the basics of Java, C, C++, Python, JavaScript and Ruby. You will certainly be discovering the specialties of this language and the areas they excel in. At the same time, you will be getting a comprehensive introduction to them so that you can jump in and start learning the language.

Before proceeding, you should remember that programming, even in the easy languages, can be difficult for the beginner. As such, you need to be patient and be ready to put in some effort so that you can succeed. As you learn, you will start finding it easier and finally make your own unique programs.

Let's us now start on the journey of programming.

Chapter 1
An Introduction To Programming

Before you start learning a particular language, you should have a proper understanding of programming. The absolute basics of programming are a must. It will help you in understanding the fundamentals of any language better.

Binary Numbers

Computers and nearly all computer based devices use the binary numeral system in their functioning. This system comprises of only two numbers, 1 and 0. Each of them is referred to as a bit. All computer programs can be simplified down to this system. In fact, the binary system has a key role in how computers store information and data of all kinds.

At the fundamental level, computers simply switch from 1 to 0 for all of their functions, no matter how simple or complex. Any data, including text and images, are stored in the computer in the form of a series of 1s and 0s. You see, computers are electrical circuits. In a circuit, an electrical current either flows in a specific line or it does. Therefore, the state can be defined as either a 1 or a 0. In other words, it is a binary situation.

Once you understand this concept, you will realize why the binary system is such basic computers. In all computers programs and situations, a problem can always be simplified down to a binary choice. As such, all computers process information using the binary system.

What is a Program?

Let us first analyze the function of a computer. Its primary function is to solve a problem. Now, how does it solve it? It does so with the help of a program. Computer programs are sequences of instructions which perform a specific task when they are executed by the computer.

No matter what the computer is, it will remain completely useless it has the right set of programs. If you are reading this book on a computer-based device, it is only because the device has a program that allows it do so.

What is a Programming Language?

As the name suggests, a programming language is a specialized language that is used for programming.

Now, there is a native programming language that all computers have and understand. This is referred to as machine code. Unfortunately, machine code can be extremely difficult for people to understand. Among other things, machine code is nearly always expressed in the binary system. Moreover, the machine code is unique to specific computer architecture. As a result, it is possible for two computers to use two variants of machine code.

Therefore, you need some way to communicate with the computers. This is why other programming languages exist. They act as an interface between people and the computer. With them, programs can be expressed in languages which can be understood by people easily. At the same time, the language will be common to different computer architectures. More importantly, the programs can be translated to machine code easily.

To make sure that this happens, a computer has to interpret or compile the program written in a programming language so that the program is executed. You need to understand compilation and interpretation with respect to computer programming.

For a compiled program, a complier has to be used so that the program can be translated into machine code for the computer to use. However, the source code will not be run by the computer in the case of an interpreted program. Instead, an interpreter reads each line of the program as it is running and modifies it into the machine code. Once modified, the computer executes that line of the program.

Programming languages can use either one of these approaches or both. Each of them has its own advantages when it comes to programming and software development. Generally, compiled programs can take longer to develop, but they can run faster. After all, the computer will execute a program that has already been translated. Interpreted programs take longer to run as they need to be translated every time they are executed. However, they can be written faster as the languages are generally simpler. At the same time, the entire program will not to be compiled after every modification or bug test.

Tips for Programming

When you are programming, you will be learning a lot of new things. As such, things can get confusing very quickly unless you can keep a track. In many cases, learners even forget a few basic principles about programming. Remember these details to ensure that you don't feel that you are getting in way over your head.

•　　When you are trying to develop a program, you should ensure that it can fulfill the need for which it is being created in the first place.

•　You should also make sure that your program can be easily used by other people.

•　You must be ready to invest a significant amount of time while learning programming.

•　On the other hand, you need to make sure that your program can be understood, improved and fixed in a short period of time.

•　Before starting a program, check out the other programs that are similar to what you want to create. Understand those programs and find out what their strong and weak points are.

You should think of ways through which the program can be improved.

• You need to plan what you want your program to be capable of before you start writing it. You can create a flowchart of the functions and features of the program beforehand.

• If possible, try to discover some good source code for programs that are similar to yours. Make sure of the quality of the code.

• When writing a program, you need to maximize the functionality while decreasing the complexity. This is the way you create a truly effective program.

• You should develop your program in such a way that it is possible to understand what is happening by simply taking a look at the source code.

• You should add comments whenever you are attempting the complicated of the program. This can be helpful for you in the long run.

• When defining variables, you must always use names that are easily understood and simple. This helps you to keep track of them and the functions that they will be used in.

You should now have an idea of what programming is like. Now, it is time to select which programming language you should try out.

Chapter 2
Go Old School With C And C++

Both C and C++ have a rich history as programming languages. C was developed in the early 1970s, and it has gone from strength to strength while C++ came about later in the 1980s.

You need to remember that both of these languages have been present in the early days of computer programming. As such, they are considered among the most foundational programming languages in the world. Therefore, you are sure to benefit greatly by learning them even if you do not use them later. In fact, learning them is like gaining an invaluable insight into the very beginnings of computer programming.

There are advantages and disadvantages to each language certainly. Nonetheless, you will gain a better understanding of programming in general. In fact, you may even find it easier to start learning other programming languages such as Java. After all, the features of C and C++ have served as an inspiration for quite a few languages.

Of course, there is a question of choice between C and C++. Now, C is the older of the two and C++ is considered to be a subset of the earlier language. C++ is also considered to be the easier of the two by many programmers. On the other hand, knowledge of C can prove to be helpful if you are hoping to become a professional programmer. Nonetheless, it is quite possible to learn C after learning C++ and vice versa.

The Design of C

C is a procedural programming language, and it was designed so as to be compiled with a relatively straightforward compiler. Its design also provides language constructs that can be mapped efficiently to machine instructions. The runtime support required is also minimal. These features enabled C to become useful for a variety of applications which had to be coded with assembly language previously.

In spite of the low-level capabilities of C, this programming language was meant to encourage programming on a cross-platform level. It is possible to compile a C program for a range of operating systems and computer platforms along as it is portably written and is standards-compliant.

A Simple Program in C

In order to illustrate the programming language of C, it helps if you have an example to look at. Here is a simple 'Hello World' program written in this language.

#include <stdio.h>

intmain ()

{

Printf ("Hello world\n");

Return 0;

}

To better understand what is happening in the program, it helps to break it up into different sections and tackle them one by one.

#include<stdio.h>

This code tells the program to include a file named 'stdio.h'which stands for Standard Input/ Output header file. With it, it is possible to use specific commands for input or output in the program. In this example, it allows us to output a message and print it on the screen.

Intmain ()

The int is known as the return value, and it is of the type integer in this example. The next part is the main () which is the main function. Every program in C has to have only one main function, and it is also the starting point for all programs.

Printf ("Hello World\n");

The printf command is used when things need to be printed on the screen which is 'Hello World' in this program. The data which is going to be printed have to place inside round brackets. In this case, 'Hello World' is placed inside inverted commas as it is a string and strings have to be placed inside inverted commas. The last part of the command is \n and it is known as an escape sequence. The \n symbolizes a newline character, and it allows the next output to be printed on the next line. There are other kinds of escape sequences which you will learn during C programming.

Return 0;

In the second line of the program, 'intmain ()' was written to denote that the main function has to return an integer. By using the 'return 0' command, the value null will be returned to the operating system. By returning a zero, you are simply telling the OS that no errors occurred when running the program.

Based on this example, there are a few things you should know about programming in this language.

- All programs written should have a single main function.

- The execution of the program will always start from the main function.

- The execution of the program will always start at the opening brace of the function and stop at the closing brace. Braces can be used to group together statements.

- Typically, all statements are written in lowercase letters in C.

- Uppercase letters are reserved for messages, output strings, and symbolic names

- You must declare a variable with the right data type before using it.

- All statements in C have to end with a semicolon.

Data Types in C

In C, you will find a standard set of fundamental data types. Due to their simplicity, they are often referred to as primitive data types. However, it is possible to develop a range of complex data structures from them. There are a total of four basic data types:

- Character - char

- Integer - int

- Floating-point - float

- double floating-point - double

The actual range and size of the data types may vary among compiles and processor types. It is possible to modify the behavior of the variable type to which they are applied with the help of data type qualifiers. There are a few qualifiers in C.

Size qualifiers can change the size of the data type. Two size qualifiers are present in C. They are 'short' and 'long'. They simply change the size of the declared variable.

Sign qualifiers determine what kind of numbers that the variable can hold. The 'signed' qualifier denotes that the variable can contain positive as well as negative numbers. However, an 'unsigned' variable can only contain positive numbers. It is not necessary to declare a variable assigned as variables are signed by default. These qualifiers can be applied to the char and int data types.

The constant qualifier is used to declare that the value of an identifier will remain unchanged in the program. In other words, its value is constant. The keyword for this qualifier is 'const'. If you want the value of a variable to be changed by external sources, you can declare it to be 'volatile'. This is another variable that you should become familiar with.

Variables

As you may know, variables are a specific location in the memory where data is stored by a program. The size of the memory block depends on the type of the variable. For identifying the memory block, you need to assign a unique name to each variable. Before variables can be used, they need to be declared with their data type and name. The syntax for variable declaration in C is given below.

[Storage-class] type data variable name [= initial value];

You do not have to define the initial value or the storage class for the variable if they are not required. It is possible to declare multiple variables at the same time as long as you want them to have the same storage class and data type. The syntax to do so is given below.

[Storage-class] type data variable name [= initial value] variable [= initial value];

Statements

In C, statements allow you to control the flow of the execution of your program. The C programming language offers you a variety of statements. Some of the most commonly used statements are given below.

- If statement

- goto statement

- switch statement

- while statement

- do-while statement

- For statement

As you proceed with programming in C, you will come across many other concepts such as input and output functions, arrays, structure, pointers and so on. Once you know about them, you can easily jump into other programming languages such as C++ and Java.

When you are writing software or applications, you will need to use Loops. This is an essential technique prevalent in all programming languages. A loop can be defined as a sequence of instructions which are repeated continually till a certain predefined condition is met. In simple terms, a block of code is repeated a set number of times till a condition are fulfilled.

Generally in a loop, a certain process is performed. This can be as simple as fetching a specific data item and modifying it. After it, a condition is checked. For example, a counter can be checked to see if it has reached a specific number. If the number has not been reached, the next instruction for the program is to return to the very first instruction of the sequence. As such, the sequence is repeated. Once the condition has been fulfilled, the instruction will cause the program to proceed to the next set of sequential instructions. It can also branch out from the loop.

There is a special kind of loop known as an infinite loop. In this loop, there is an absence of a functioning exit instruction. As a result, the loop will repeat continually till it is sensed by the operating system which will terminate the program and an error will show. The infinite loop can also be stopped due to the occurrence of some other event. For example, the program can be made to terminate automatically after a specific duration of time.

In C#, you will come across four different kinds of loops. As such, you need to be familiar with them.

The while Loop

The simplest of the four loops in C# is the while loop. In this type of loop, a sequence of instructions will be executed continually as long as the defined condition returns true. It will only exit when the condition returns false. Here is an example to help you understand it.

```csharp
using System;

namespace ConsoleApplication1

{

    class Program

    {

        static void Main(string[] args)

        {

            Int number = 0;

            while (number < 10)

            {

                Console.WriteLine (number);

                number = number + 1;

            }

            Console.ReadLine ();

        }

    }

}
```

When you run this code, you will find that the program lists a sequence of numbers in the console starting at 0 and ending at 10.

Of course, the variable number is first defined as 0. Every time that the loop is executed, the variable is incremented by 1. You can see this happening in this statement:

number = number + 1

As a result, the program keeps displaying the numbers till it reaches nine which is the last thing to be displayed. You may be wondering why nine is being displayed when you have mentioned 10 in the code.

The condition will only be true when the number is less than 10. Once the number becomes 10, the condition becomes false. After all, ten is not less than 10. As you can see, the condition of the while loop is checked before the program enters the loop sequence. Once the number turns 10, the condition becomes false, and the while loop sequence is not executed.

The do Loop

The do loop shares certain similarities with the while loop with one major difference. The while loop checks the condition before the loop sequence is executed. On the other hand, the do loop will check the condition after the loop has been executed. This means the loop sequence will always be executed at least one time before exiting. This is not possible with the while loop. Take a look at the following example.

```
using System;

namespace ConsoleApplication1

{

  class Program

  {

    static void Main(string[] args)

    {

      Int number = 0;

      do

      {

        Console.WriteLine (number);

        number = number + 1;

      } while (number < 10)

      Console.ReadLine ();

    }

  }
```

```
}
```

On running this program, you will see the numbers being displayed from 0 to 9. Once the number becomes 10 or more than 10, the program will exit the loop sequence. As you can see, the do loop functions in a similar manner to the while loop but checks the condition after the execution of a sequence.

The for Loop

The for loop is different from that of the do or the while loops. The for loop is generally used when you know the exact number of iterations that you want. It can also be used when you have defined a variable that contains the amount. The following example illustrates the use of the for loop.

```
using System;

namespace ConsoleApplication1

{

    class Program

    {

        static void Main(string[] args)

        {

            Int number = 10;

            for (Int i = 0; i < number; i++)
```

```
Console.WriteLine (i);

Console.ReadLine ();

    }

  }

}
```

When you run this program, you will find that the output is the same as that of the previous examples. However, the for loop tends to be more compact than the while, and the do loops, as you can see.

There are three parts to the for loop. First, a variable is initialized for counting. Then, a conditional statement is defined to test the variable. Finally, we increment the counter variable. In C# and a few other programming languages, you can use ++ instead of writing the entire statement: "variable = variable + 1" The result will be the same.

The first section will be executed only once before the actual loop starts. This is the section where the variable i is defined and then set to 0. The next two sections will be executed for each iteration of the for loop. In each repetition, the variable I will be compared to the number variable. When the variable i is less than the number variable, the loop will run once again. After the execution, the variable I will be increased by 1. In this case, it will continue to loop till variable I become equal to 10.

The for each Loop

The for each loop is quite different from the previous three loops. This loop operates on a collection of items. Arrays or other kinds of built-in list types can also be used. For the following example, an ArrayList is used as it is one of the simple lists available in C#. ArrayList tends to work in a similar to an array.

```
using System;

Using System.Collections;

namespace ConsoleApplication1

{

  class Program

  {

    static void Main(string[] args)

    {

      ArrayList list = new ArrayList ();

      list.Add ("Dog");

      list.Add ("Cat");

      list.Add ("Bird");
```

```
        foreach (string name in list)

            Console.WriteLine (name);

        Console.ReadLine ();

    }

  }

}
```

As you can see, an instance of an ArrayList is created first in the code. This is followed by the addition of a few string items to the list. In this example, we have added a few names of animals as string items to the ArrayList list.

The foreach loop is then used to run through each of the items. In each repetition, the name variable is set to the item that has been reached in the ArrayList. This variable is then pushed for output. As a result, you can see the animals that were inserted into the ArrayList being displayed on the console

It is vital that you inform the foreach loop as to which data type you are looking to take out of the collection. In this case, we have specified that the name variable will belong to the string data type. It is possible that you have a list of different data types. In such cases, you can use the object class rather than a specific class so as to take out each item of the list as an object.

If you are going to be using collections in your programs, you will find the foreach loop to be the best choice among all the loop types available in C#. This is mainly because the foreach is simpler than all of the other loops when it comes to such operations.

Chapter 3
Enjoy The Versatility Of Java

Java is one of the most influential programming languages in the world. It also remained popular and pervasive in the computing world. You can discover Java being used on all kinds of platforms, from the web to operating systems and even devices. You will find Java to be filled with features. As a programming language, it is class based and object oriented. It has been designed to be portable so that you can work on it on a wide variety of platforms. This is why it is still popular all over the world even two decades after its initial release.

On the other hand, Java can be difficult to understand at times and hard to program efficiently and effectively. However, its popularity means that you will not lack for resources to help you understand or avenues to explore as a programmer. Another benefit of learning Java is that it forces you to think analytically and logically. In other words, you will start thinking like a programmer. You can get a better understanding of how computers process information as well. The core concepts and fundamentals that you learn in Java will prove to be useful when you start learning other programming languages.

The Features of Java

Java was originally developed in 1991 by Sun Microsystems Inc. Now, it is maintained by Oracle Corporation who acquired Sun Microsystems in 2009. Its popularity hinges on its excellent features.

• **Platform Independence:** Unlike some other programming languages, Java is platform independent. As a result, you can run Java programs on all platforms no matter which platform you compiled them on.

• **Object Oriented:** While Java is an object oriented programming language, it lacks some complex features such as multiple inheritances, operator overloading, and explicit memory allocation. As a result, it is a simple language to learn.

• **Strong Language:** Mishandled runtime errors and memory management are two of the main issues that result in program failures. In Java, these issues can be efficiently taken care of. Exception handling procedures can resolve mishandled runtime errors while garbage collection can take care of memory management mistakes.

• **Security:** When writing Java programs, all codes will remain confined inside the Java Runtime Environment. As a result, unauthorized access to the system resources is not granted.

- **Multithreading:** Due to its support for multithreading, Java allows your program to perform different tasks at the same time.

A Simple Program in Java

To gain a better understanding of what Java is like, the following example will be of help. This is a Hello World program, a simple program that is often used for illustrating the basics of a programming language. You will already have come across such an example in the chapter on C and C++.

Public class Main {

Public static void main (String [] args) {

System.out.println ("Hello, World!");

* }*

}

Now, let us examining each section of the program to understand what the functions and keywords are and what they do.

Public class Main {

This is the first line of the program, and it defines a class called Main. If you want a line of code to run in a Java program, you have to place it inside a class. Here the class Main is declared. It has been defined as public. Therefore, other classes can access it. You should also remember that a public class must be declared inside a file which has the same name. In this case, the name of the file should be Main.java. If you do not do so, you will get an error during compilation.

Public static void main (String [] args) {

This is the starting point of the Java program. It is necessary for the main method to have the exact signature shown so that the program can be run. Here are a few of the keywords that you need to take a look into. You are already familiar with public, and the others will be discussed shortly. 'Main' is, of course, the name of the method.

System.out.println ("Hello, World!");

The system is a predefined class in Java, and it contains some variables and methods which are useful while programming. The next keyword is out, and it is a static variable from System. It is representative of the program output. PrintIn is a method found inside out and it is used for printing a line.

Datatypes and Variables in Java

In Java, there are three kinds of variables and several data types. Understanding them is vital when you want to write programs in this language.

Data Types

There are two kinds of data types in Java, primitive and non-primitive. Primitive data types are predefined and provided by

Java. Some examples of these in Java include Boolean, char, int, long, short and float. On the other hand, non-primitive data types are not defined by Java. Instead, they will be created by you, the programmer. They refer to a memory location which is why they are sometimes known as reference variables. String and array are some of the non-primitive data types.

Variables

In Java, there are three kinds of variables that you can use for your programs. The type depends on how you declare the variable. Local variables are those which are declared inside a method. On the other hand, instance variables are defined outside the method but inside the class. Static variables are simply those variables that are declared with the static keyword, and they cannot be local variables. You will learn about these uses when you start programming in Java in earnest.

As with other programming languages, you need to declare a variable before it can be used. The basic syntax for declaring a variable in Java is given below.

Data type variable [= value];

You can declare multiple variables of the samedatatype in a single statement. You just need to use a comma to separate them.

In Java, you need to take care when you are declaring variables as there are rules in place for it. The names for variables are case-sensitive. Therefore, 'Hi' and 'hi' will be considered as two separate variables. In fact, it is a good practice to avoid starting variable names with capitals as such a format is usually applied to class names. You can use the '$' and '_' signs but use them intelligently. Whitespace is not allowed in variable names, and you cannot start a name with a number. Finally, you cannot use a reserved word or keyword as a variable name.

Loops and Conditional Statements

In a program, statements and lines of codes are executed in a sequential manner. However, it is possible to create complex execution paths to make certain programs and functions possible. This is achieved by means of different control structures such as conditional statements and loops.

Loops

A loop statement is used when a block of code needs to be executed multiple times. There are different kinds of loop statements available in Java for specific situations. They are listed as follows.

- **While loop:** This will cause a group of statements to be repeated as long as a given condition remains true. Once the condition becomes false, the loop will no longer be executed. The condition will be tested before the loop is executed.

- **Do-While loop:** This loop works in a similar manner to the while loop. However, it will check the condition after the code in the loop has been executed.

- **For loop:** Here, a block of code will be executed a set number of times. It allows the code which manages the variable for the loop to be shortened.

Conditional Statements

These are actually structures that are accompanied by one or multiple conditions. Those conditions are evaluated by the program and the statements executed according to the result of the evaluation. If the condition is true, a specific statement or set of statements will be executed. If false, another set of statements will be executed. In other words, these structures allow the program to make decisions. Java offers a few kinds of conditional structures to be used.

- **If statement:** This contains a Boolean expression along with the statements that are to be executed when the condition is true.

- **If else statement:** This is a regular if statement used alongside an else statement. If the condition is false, the statements listed under the else statement will be executed. The code under the if statement is executed when it returns true.

- **Nested if statements:** This is a special use of the if statement. It is possible to nest if statements inside one another. It is also applicable for if else statements.

- **Switch statement:** This statement used to test a variable for equality against a specified list of values. Each value will have a statement or block of code that will be executed when the value of the variable matches it.

These are some of the basics that you should be familiar with when you are learning how to develop programs using the Java language. As mentioned earlier, Java is an excellent stepping stone to the world of programming. Once learned, you will find it easier to learn other languages.

Advantages Offered by JavaScript

JavaScript offers a range of benefits to the users. Some of them are given below.

Simplicity: JavaScript, like HTML and CSS, is quite easy to learn. Moreover, you can also start implementing JavaScript code with equal ease.

Speed: JavaScript is executed on the client-side. As a result, all code functions can be executed immediately. There is no need to contact the server and then wait for a response. This allows JavaScript to be quite fast.

Versatility: JavaScript is compatibility with quite a few other languages. It is, in fact, possible to insert JavaScript into any web page irrespective of its file extension. You can also use JavaScript inside scripts that have been written in PHP, Perl and other languages. Therefore, JavaScript can be used in a wide range of applications.

API Availability: The availability of Application Programming Interfaces, or APIs for short, provides JavaScript with a range of functionality. This includes the setting of CSS styles, generation of audio samples and dynamic creation of HTML among others. While these APIs are built into the different web browsers, third-party APIs are also available which allow you to incorporate functionality from other web properties such as social networks like Facebook.

The Hello World Example in JavaScript

Here is the hello world example in JavaScript. This will illustrate how the language works and familiarize you with the syntax as well. As you will see, the language is quite simple.

```
<Html>

<Body>

<script language="javascript" type="text/javascript">

<!--

        document.write ("Hello World!")

    //-->

</script>

</body>

</html>
```

The Syntax in JavaScript

JavaScript is supposed to be implemented with the help of JavaScript statements. These statements are placed inside the <script>... </script> HTML tags in a web page. The <script> tags can be placed anywhere within the HTML document. The <script> tag will alert the browser to interpret the text between the tags as a script. An example of the JavaScript syntax is given below.

<script language="javascript" type="text/javascript">

Code in JavaScript

</script>

The script tag has two crucial attributes. They are given below.

Language: This attribute is used to specify which scripting language is being used. Of course, since you are using JavaScript, the value of this attribute is javascript. On the other hand, this attribute is rarely used these days for the recent versions of HTML and XHTML.

Type: This attribute is now currently being used for indicating the scripting language. The value of this attribute should be set as 'text/javascript'.

Line Breaks and Whitespace

JavaScript will ignore whitespaces. Therefore, you use newlines, tabs and spaces in your scripts freely. Of course, you should be using them to format your programs and make them look consistent and neat. This allows the code to be read and understood easily.

Semicolons

Generally, semicolons are used to mark the end of statements. This is the case in languages like Java, C++ and C. However, JavaScript makes semicolons optional in one condition. You need to ensure that each statement has been placed on a separate line. As long as you meet this condition, you can avoid inserting semicolons in the code. However, using semicolons is a good practice especially when you are learning to program.

Case Sensitivity

You need to ensure the proper uses of cases in JavaScript as this language is case-sensitive. Therefore, all keywords, function names, variables and other identifiers must be typed with the correct case. Consistency is vital. In JavaScript, the identifiers hi and HI will have different meanings.

How to Place JavaScript in HTML Documents?

One of the good things about JavaScript is that you have the flexibility to add the code anywhere you want in an HTML document. Nonetheless, it is an excellent idea to follow the preferred methods. This can improve the readability and execution of the JavaScript code in the HTML document. Here are the best ways to include JavaScript in HTML.

Inside the <head> tags

This option is generally used when you want the script to run when an event takes place. For example, you may want the script to run when the user clicks something somewhere. In these situations, the script will be placed inside the <head> tags as shown in the following example.

<Html>

<Head>

<script type="text/javascript">

<!--

     Function sayHello () {

     Alert ("Hello World")

     }

     //-->

</script>

</head>

<Body>

<input type="button" onclick="sayHello ()" value="Say Hello" />

</body>

</html>

Inside the <body> tags

In some cases, you may need the script to run while the page loads. This is done to allow the script to generate the content located in the page. In this case, the script will have to be placed inside the <body> tags. In this method, you will not have any function that has been defined with JavaScript. You can see the example given below for such an inclusion of JavaScript.

<Html>

<Head>

</head>

<Body>

<script type="text/javascript">

<!--

  document.write ("Hello World")

  //-->

</script>

<p>Web Page Body </p>

</body>

</html>

Inside the <head> and <body> tags

If you want, you can combine the two methods above. In other words, you can place your JavaScript code inside both, the <head> and the <body> tags, in the same document. Check out the example given below to see how it works.

<Html>

<Head>

<script type="text/javascript">

<!--

Function sayHello () {

Alert ("Hello World")

}

//-->

</script>

</head>

<Body>

<script type="text/javascript">

<!--

document.write ("Hello World")

```
//-->
```

```
</script>
```

```
<input type="button" onclick="sayHello ()" value="Say Hello"
/>
```

```
</body>
```

```
</html>
```

Inside an External File

Including JavaScript inside the HTML document is a good idea when you are creating simple web pages. However, as you create websites or complex web pages, it is possible that you can find yourself reusing the same JavaScript code in multiple locations. You may even end up using the same code in multiple web pages.

As you have seen in CSS, it is possible for you to create an entirely separate file to keep your JavaScript code. You can put in all the JavaScript code that needs to be used in multiple locations or web pages inside an external file. That file should have the '.js.' extension and be associated with the web pages that require the code. The following example illustrates how an external JavaScript file can be included in an HTML document. In this example, filename.js is the file used for containing the JavaScript code.

```
<Html>
```

```
<Head>

<script type="text/javascript" src="filename.js" ></script>

</head>

<Body>

    .......

</body>

</html>
```

Data types and Variables in JavaScript

In any programming language, data types and variables are considered to be fundamental to its operation. Here is a short introduction to the data types and variables as used in JavaScript.

Data types

As you may already know, data types denote the kind of values that can be used in a programming language. There are three primitive data types available in JavaScript as mentioned below.

- Numbers

- Boolean

- Text Strings

There are two trivial data types available in JavaScript. They are undefined and null. Each of them defines a single value only.

In JavaScript, there is no difference between floating-point values and integer values. Instead, all numbers are considered to be floating-point values in JavaScript.

Variables

As you already know, variables are containers in which data can be stored. In JavaScript, a variable must be declared before it can be used in the program. You can use the var keyword to declare a variable. Look at the following example to understand how it works.

```
<script type="text/javascript">

<!--

    Var money;

    Var name;

//-->

</script>
```

In the above example, the var keyword has been used twice for declaring two variables, money and name. However, JavaScript allows multiple variables to be declared with just one var keyword. You can see this happening in the following example.

```
<script type="text/javascript">

<!--
```

Var money, name;

//-->

</script>

Variable initialization takes place when a value is stored in a variable. It is possible to perform variable initialization while declaring the variable in JavaScript. Alternatively, you can initialize the variable later when you require that variable. You can see this happening in the following example.

<script type="text/javascript">

<!--

Var name = "John";

Var money;

Money = 12.30;

//-->

</script>

When using variables, there are two things that you need to keep in mind.

• The var keyword must be used either for declaration or initialization. As such, it will be used only once in the lifespan of any variable in a single program. The same variable must never be declared twice, or it can result in errors.

• As JavaScript is an untied language, a variable can hold any value irrespective of the data type. In other words, you do not have to mention what kind of value that a variable should contain while it is being declared. You can change the value type of the variable during the execution. JavaScript will handle it automatically.

The Scope of Variables in JavaScript

The variable scope refers to the section of the program in which the variable is defined. Variables in JavaScript can have either one of two scopes.

Global Variables: These variables can be defined anywhere in your code due to its global scope.

Local Variables: These variables exist only inside the function that it has been defined in. Function parameters will always be local to that specific function.

In JavaScript, a local variable will be given precedence inside the body of the function if there is a global variable that has the same name. By declaring a local variable that has the same name as that of a global variable, you are effectively hiding that global variable in the function.

Rules for Variable Names

When you are giving names to your variables, you need to remember the following rules.

- The reserved keywords in JavaScript cannot be used as names for your variables.

- Variable names cannot start with a number in JavaScript. They must either start with a letter or underscore.

- As mentioned earlier, JavaScript is case sensitive. Therefore, the variable names must be used accordingly.

Events in JavaScript

An event is an action that causes a JavaScript code to be executed. Events are generally triggered by the users. For example, the click of a mouse can be an event. Based on the events, it is possible to code a response in JavaScript. For example, displaying a message can be a response to an event. These responses can be said to be the event handlers as they handle the event taking place. In JavaScript, it is possible to classify events in a number of ways. After all, there are a huge number of them.

The onClick event

The most common event type is the onClick event. This takes place whenever the user left-clicks the webpage. Against this event, you can make the appropriate response such as displaying a message or putting your validation. The following example illustrates the use of such an event for displaying a message.

<Html>

<Head>

```
<script type="text/javascript">

<!--

        Function sayHello () {

        Alert ("Hello World")

        }

        //-->

</script>

</head>

<Body>

<p>Click the following button and see result</p>

<Form>

<input type="button" onclick="sayHello ()" value="Say Hello" />

</form>

</body>

</html>
```

Conditional Statements in JavaScript

Like other programming languages, there are different kinds of conditional statements available in JavaScript. They allow you to define a condition whose results determine the action that will be done. They allow your program to make a decision based on the outcome of the condition and perform the relevant action.

If...else statement

One of the simplest and a very common conditional statement in JavaScript is the if else statement. This statement can be used in different forms.

• **If statement:** In this statement, the code will only be executed when the condition expression gives a result of true.

• **If...else statement:** Here, there will be two codes. The code under the if statement will be executed when the condition is true while the code under the else statement will be executed when the condition returns false.

• **If...else if statement:** In this statement, multiple conditions are checked instead of a single one. The condition that returns true will be executed.

The basic syntax for the if...else statement is given below.

If (expression) {

   Statement(s) to be executed if expression is true

}

Looping in JavaScript

Looping allows you to execute a single block of code multiple times till a given condition is met. JavaScript offers two kinds of loops, the for loop and the while loop.

The for loop

The for loop allows the same block of code statements to be repeatedly executed till a certain specified condition is met. The syntax of the for loop is given as follows.

For (initial expression; condition expression; loop expression)

{Statements}

The while loop

With the while loop, it becomes possible to control the number of times the loop is executed. In other words, this loop is used when you know the number of times a loop needs to be executed. As such, you need to make sure that loop is written properly so that it does not get repeated infinitely. The syntax of the while loop is given below.

While (expression) {

*   Statement(s) to be executed if expression is true*

}

Being an entire language, JavaScript offers a lot of other features and functions. However, you will be getting to them with time as you learn JavaScript in greater detail. Of course, you should now know how to implement a basic script written in JavaScript in your HTML web page.

Chapter 4
Build The Web With JavaScript

First of all, you should confuse JavaScript with Java. They are completely separate programming languages with no links to each other. It was originally developed in the 90s. JavaScript is one of the most necessary technologies in the development of the web as it is in use today. However, this programming language is also used in places other than a web browser such as connected services and applications.

As a programming language, JavaScript is dynamic. As a result, you have the flexibility to utilize an object-oriented programming approach or imperative and functional ones although the language is mainly object oriented. If you are already familiar with C, you will find JavaScript easier as much of the syntax is derived from the earlier programming language. In fact, it is quite easy to pick up this language. At the same time, knowledge of JavaScript can make it easier to learn Java and C.

Moreover, it is becoming very popular these days. If you are planning to become a professional coder or build things for the internet, JavaScript is one of the best languages to start with.

You will be able to start building web programs quickly on learning this language.

The Features of JavaScript

JavaScript is capable of adding a variety of beautiful effects to a webpage among other things. When you are learning this programming language, it helps to understand what its features are. Here are some of the most important ones.

Browser Support

JavaScript has been accepted by all browsers as a standard scripting language. As a result, there is no need to install any plug-in to start using JavaScript in your browser, unlike Flash. More importantly, browsers provide integrated support to this language.

Client Side and Server Side Together

JavaScript can access the Document object model of a browser. As a result, it is possible to modify the structure of the WebPages at runtime. As a result, you can use this language for the addition of a variety of effects to the WebPages. At the same time, it is possible to use it on the server side. One such use is the creation of web scripts.

Scripting vs. Programming with JavaScript

JavaScript is often referred to as a scripting language because that is exactly what it is. It is not exactly a programming language per se. After all, the web browser does a lot of the work involved in the program. Since the browser does the actual work, it is possible to make changes by writing a few lines of code, which is relatively easier. This is why JavaScript is considered to be an easy language for beginners.

Nonetheless, there are some complicated aspects of this language. Even though it is employed as a scripting language, JavaScript is a thorough programming language. You can be certain write complex programs with it. Of course, this is rarely required when you are creating WebPages.

Writing a Simple Program in JavaScript

To get a better idea of JavaScript as a language, you should start writing your very first program in. The staple 'Hello World' example will be used in this case as well. The good thing is that it is very easy to write this program in JavaScript.

Before you can start, you will need to fulfill some basic requirements. One advantage of JavaScript is that it can be easily interpreted by the browser itself. As a result, you do not require any additional software or compilers for writing programs in this language. The only things you need are given below.

•   **Text Editor:** You can use Notepad for writing the program. However, you should consider getting Notepad++ which is an invaluable text editor for programmers. You can get this application for free.

- **Web Browser:** You can choose any browser that you are comfortable with as all of them support JavaScript.

There is one more thing you need to do before you write the actual program and that is to create the HTML Framework. Generally, JavaScript programs will be embedded in the web page. In other words, they are written alongside the HTML. However, it is possible to include the programs externally. As such, a simply HTML file will have to be created for including the JavaScript.

To do so, open the text editor of your choice and type the following lines in the file.

<! DOCTYPE HTML>

<Html>

<Head>

<Title>JavaScript Hello World</title>

</head>

<Body>

<h1>JavaScript Hello World Example</h1>

</body>

</html>

Once done, you can save this file with a name of your choice but make sure that the file type has been designated as an HTML file. That means the file's extension should be .html and nothing else. You now have the basic template ready.

As such, you can insert the JavaScript code into the file now. Open it up and add the following lines to it. Make sure that they have been mentioned after the <h1> tag.

<Script>

<alert ("Hello World!")

<Script>

Save the file and your JavaScript program is finally ready. You can now use your web browser to run the program. Open the file in the web browser and you will see the message, 'Hello World!' being displayed.

Understanding the Syntax in JavaScript

Like all programming languages, JavaScript has its own syntax that you need to follow when writing code with it. Here are some of the most important parts of the JavaScript syntax.

<Script>

When you want to implement statements in JavaScript, you need to apply the above tag. All statements have to be placed between <script> and </script> in a web page for them to be executed. It is possible to place the <script> tags with the

JavaScript code anywhere you want in a web page. However, it is a good practice to place them inside the <head> tags. The function of the <script> tag is to alert the browser to ensure that all the text between those tags is interpreted as a script. There are two important attributes to the <script> tag.

•	**Language:** The language attribute will specify which scripting language is being used. Generally, the value of this attribute is JavaScript. On the other hand, the latest versions of HTML and XHTML have made it unnecessary to use this attribute.

•	**Type:** Nowadays, the type attribute is recommended when you wish to mention which scripting language is being used. You should set its value to *'text/JavaScript'*.

Line Breaks and Whitespace

Unlike other programming languages, JavaScript does not pay attention to spaces, newlines, and tabs in its programs. Since they are ignored, you can use these breaks and white spaces as many times as you want without breaking the program. You can freely use them to format the programs to make the code look neat so that it can be read and understood in an easy manner.

Semicolons are Discretional

In most programming languages such as Java and C, simple statements end with a semicolon. This is also the case in JavaScript with a major difference. They are optional in JavaScript as long as the statements are placed on separate lines. You must use semicolons when you are placing two statements in one line. Be that as it may, using semicolons is a good practice for beginners.

Case Sensitivity in JavaScript

JavaScript is sensitive to the cases of the words. In other words, 'Hi' and 'hi' will be treated differently by the language.

Datatypes and Variables

Like with other programming languages, it is important to understand data types and variables in JavaScript.

Data Types

JavaScript offers three different primitive data types. They are Numbers, Strings of text and Boolean. The Numbers data type represents both integers and floating-point. The programming language does not define them as separate data types. Instead, all numbers will be represented as floating-point values.

There are also two other data types in JavaScript. They are undefined and null. Each of these trivial data types defines a single value only. There is a composite data type in JavaScript as well, and it is called object.

Variables

As is the case with other programming languages, there are variables in JavaScript. They need to be declared before they can be used in the program. In JavaScript, the variables have to be declared with the help of the 'var' keyword. It is possible to declare multiple variables in a single statement with this keyword. The syntax for declaring a variable is given below.

Var money;

Variable initialization is quite easy in JavaScript. You can store a value in a variable as soon as it has been declared or you can do it later in the program when required. You should remember that the 'var' keyword can be used only once for a specific variable in a program.

Another thing about JavaScript is that it is an untyped language. Therefore, a variable can contain any value irrespective of its data type in JavaScript. In other words, you do not have to inform the program what kind of data the variable can hold during its declaration. Moreover, it is possible to change the value type of any variable later. JavaScript will automatically handle the changes during the execution of the program.

In JavaScript, a variable can have two different scopes. The scope defines the region of a program in which the variable is defined.

• **Local Variables:** A local variable will remain visible only inside the function where the variable has been defined in. Function parameters are always kept local to that specific function.

- **Global Variables:** These variables have a global scope. In other words, it can be defined anywhere you want in the code of the program.

You should remember that a local variable will be given precedence in a function over a global variable that has the same name. If you declare a local variable with a name inside the body of a function that is shared by a global variable, you will be hiding the global variable for that function.

As you keep learning JavaScript, you will be coming across various functions, loops, and events. Once you can master this programming language, you can seek jobs as a web developer at the very least. Alternatively, you can pick up quite a few other programming languages more easily than before

Chapter 5
Learn The Incredible Language Of Python

Python is often mentioned as one of the best programming languages for a beginner to start with. If you are an absolute newcomer to programming, this can be an excellent choice for you. Python is quite an old language having been developed in the 80s. Guido van Rossum who developed it later gave away the language as open source. It is currently taken care of by the Python Software Foundation. Python can be used freely even for commercial applications

This is generally used as a scripting language with which programmers can compose large amounts of code in a very short period of time. Of course, the code will still remain functional and easily readable. Due to its flexibility, this language is one of the most popular of all the high-level languages in use today.

However, there is one thing you must know about Python. You are not going to be starting at the basic level even when you are a beginner. On the other hand, you will be learning a number of useful things such as modularity, naming conventions and indentation, all of which can make it easier for you when you learn other programming languages. Another advantage of this language is that the developer community is thriving allowing you to get a range of resources to help you learn Python.

Features of Python

Python is quite a powerful object-oriented programming language. It has some excellent features to offer to the programmer

• **Ease:** The ease of using Python showcases itself in multiple ways. There are fewer keywords in this language along with a clear syntax and simple structure. As a result, it is easy to learn it. The code here can be read quite easily as it is clearly defined.

• **Portability:** It is possible to run this language on a range of hardware platforms. At the same time, it will have the same interface on all of them.

• **Extendibility:** It is possible to add low-level modules to the interpreter in Python. With them, you can customize your tools or add new functions so that the tools become more efficient.

• **GUI Programming:** One of the best things about Python is that it can support GUI applications. These can be created and then ported to many windows systems and system calls including Macintosh and UNIX's X Window system.

• **Scalability:** With Python, you get a better support and structure for larger programs.

• **Interactive Mode:** In Python, you can get an interactive mode. It enables interactive debugging and testing of your code snippets easily.

- **Multiple Approaches:** While Python is mainly an object oriented programming language, it is possible to use other programming approaches such as structured and functional.

- **Other Features:** Python offers very high-level dynamic data types. Apart from supporting dynamic type checking, it also offers automatic garbage collection. Moreover, you can integrate Python with other programming languages such Java, C++ and C easily.

A Simple Program in Python

Before you can write a Python program, you need to install it on your computer. You will also get a program called IDLE. This is short for Integrated Development Environment. This is known as IDE for short in other programming languages. IDLE looks a lot similar to a basic text editor. On opening IDLE, you need to put in the following command at the prompt.

print ("Hello, World!")

As you can see, the code for a Hello World program in Python is much shorter than the other programming languages that you have seen so far. This is one of the reasons for the popularity of this language. You can even easily understand what is happening in the code.

Data Types and Variables

Understanding the variables and data types will certainly help you out when you are learning Python.

Data Types

In Python, all values have a data type. Moreover, everything is considered to be an object in this programming language. Therefore, data types are actually considered to be classes while variables are considered to be instances of the respective classes. Here are some of the most important data types in Python.

•   **Python Numbers:** In this category, you will find floating point numbers, complex numbers, and integers. In Python, they are defined as a float, complex, and int. It is possible to discover the class of the variable with the type () function. The *instance ()* function can be used to check whether an object belongs to a specified class.

•   **Python List:** As the name suggests, List is an ordered series of items. It is one of the most widely used data types and is rather flexible. In Python, the items of a list can belong to different data types. The value of the items in a list can be changed as per requirements. Therefore, the list is mutable.

•   **Python Tuple:** Tuple is similar to a list as it also has an ordered series of items. However, a tuple is immutable. Therefore, the values in a tuple cannot be modified once it has been created. They are mainly used for write-protecting data.

Variables

While the function of variables in Python is the same as the other programming languages, there is a difference in their declaration. In Python, you do not have to declare a variable before using it. You simply need to assign a value to the variable, and it will exist. You do not have to define the data type of the variable as well. Python will define the data type automatically based on the value assigned to the variable.

Naming the variables properly is essential in Python. The names can be a combination of letters in uppercase and smaller case along with digits and underscore. However, a name cannot start with a number. Special symbols cannot be used for naming variables. You cannot use keywords for the names as well. These rules are also applicable when you are writing identifiers.

Conditional Statements and Loops

Like other programming languages, Python also offers a range of conditional statements to help your program make decisions and loops for executing a code multiple times.

Conditional Statements

There are a few conditional statements available in Python. In this programming language, a null or a zero value is considered to be TRUE while any non-null or non-zero value is taken to be False.

• **If statements:** In this conditional statement, the block of code under the statement will be executed when the if expression returns TRUE. If FALSE, the execution of that code will be skipped and the statement after it will be executed.

- **If else statements:** These statements contain an else statement after the if statement. The block of code under the else statement will be executed when the if expression is determined to be FALSE.

- **If elif else statements:** The elif statement is used to check multiple conditions and expressions. When one of the given conditions is determined to be TRUE, a block of code associated with that elif statement will be executed. As such, there can be multiple elif statements following an if statement. The block of code executed corresponds to the elif statement which was evaluated to TRUE.

Loops

Loops in Python are similar to other programming languages.

- **While loop:** This loop allows you to repeat the execution of a block of code as long as the specified condition is TRUE. The condition will be tested every time before the body of the loop is executed.

- **For loop:** The for loop also allows you to execute a block of code. However, it keeps the code required for managing the loop variable short.

Like other programming languages, it is also possible to create nested loops in Python.

Learning Python can certainly open up a plethora of opportunities. More importantly, once you become adept in Python, you will find programming easier in general.

Nearly all of the applications that are used by a person on a daily basis communicate with various servers to work. For an application to do this successfully, it will have to be programmed correctly. If a request is not processed correctly, it will usually lead to a variety of errors. In this first chapter, we are going to cover some of the basics of programming and why they have to be learned when trying to achieve success with the program.

Breaking Down the Function of an Application

The first thing that you will need to do when trying to be a successful programmer is how to break down what an application does. To be a good Python Programmer, you will need to become familiar with the order of operations required to make a program work. The best way to get experience with this process is by making a list of what needs to work in an application and what operations have to be laid out for this to happen.

By getting familiar with this breaking down of operations, you will be able to get an application built without having complications that compromise its functionality. You need to be aware that computers are made to perform precisely what they are programmed to do. This means that if there are any mistakes, then the computer will not be able to compensate for them. Due to this fact, you will have to be meticulous in regards to the commands that you give to the computer. A computer is inflexible in regards to the way it obeys commands, which puts all of the responsibility on you to input the right Python Programming to ensure the application you design is correct.

The Special Language of Computers

The language of computers is also something that you will need to become very familiar with. You will not be able just to tell a computer to check an email or show an individual screen when a link is clicked; you have to learn how to speak their language. There have been many different types of coding used over the years, and each of them seems more complicated than the next. Using bits of binary code will help to turn parts of a computer's processor on and off with ease. The whole purpose behind Python Programming is to make it easy for you to develop applications without having to complicate matters like C++ code can do. The lines of code that are produced by Python are very easy to read and to alter when needed. When using a coding discipline like C++, a beginner will find it nearly impossible to figure out what the lines of code say and how to work within them to create what they want. The primary goal of any application is to allow users to communicate with their computers in a new way. Your job as a programmer will allow you to open up a whole new world for people when it comes to using their computers.

Things to Consider When Working on a New Application

When working on a new application, you will usually have a variety of different roadblocks to address along the way. When first starting out in the world of Python Programming, you will have a bit of a learning curve. The more you can work on various applications, the easier you will find it to become familiar with the programming process. Following a few ground rules will allow you to perfect an application without a lot of effort being invested in the process.

The first thing you need to consider when attempting to develop an application is what you find distracting about it. For most programmers, developing applications that are straightforward and easy to use is critical. By taking the time to simplify the application you are working on, you will be able to eliminate the confusion that a user may have. One of the first things that you will need to do when starting an application is to set the date and time. In order to do this, you will need to do the following:

- Open a Blank file

- Save it as dateparser.py

- Use the following code to set time and date

from datetime import datetime

now = datetime.now()

mm = str(now.month)

dd = str(now.day)

yyyy = str(now.year)

hour = str(now.hour)

mi = str(now.minute)

ss = str(now.second)

print mm + "/" + dd + "/" + yyyy + " " + hour + ":" + mi + ":" + ss

Once you have this in the file, you will need to save it and exit. Once you are ready to put these changes in your application, you will need to run it. In some cases, you may want to use the time.sleep function to provide a time break within an application. Most programmers want to use this break in 5 second intervals. Below you will find the coding you need to activate this time sleep within your application.

import time

time.sleep(5)

The number in the parenthesis is the number of seconds the time sleep will be active for. You can change this number in order to find the right delay that works for the particular part of your application. If you want to avoid having to input all of the numbers regarding time and date, the following Python coding will allow you to get the current time and date settings for your application.

```
import datetime

now = datetime.datetime.now()

print

print "Current date and time using str method of datetime object:"

print str(now)

print

print "Current date and time using instance attributes:"

print "Current year: %d" % now.year

print "Current month: %d" % now.month

print "Current day: %d" % now.day

print "Current hour: %d" % now.hour

print "Current minute: %d" % now.minute

print "Current second: %d" % now.second

print "Current microsecond: %d" % now.microsecond

print

print "Current date and time using strftime:"
```

print now.strftime("%Y-%m-%d %H:%M")

Another thing to think about when attempting to perfect an application is easy to use elements it has. Once an application has been built, you will need to give it a test run. During this trial run, you will need to think more like a user than a programmer. Be sure to make notes as to what parts of the application were easiest to use and which ones gave you trouble. By doing this type of assessment, you can fix the bugs that you find with ease.

The last thing you will need to contemplate when attempting to fine tune an application is whether or not it did the job it was intended for. If the app looks great and has impressive graphics, but does not do the job it needs to, then you will need to go back to the drawing board. The bells and whistles that are on an app will only go so far. The last thing that you want is to have people growing tired of your app after only a few uses. Having an application that is functional is far better than having a program than just looks good. There is a gray area that will allow you to have both of these elements. Your job is to find this middle ground and use it to your advantage.

Reasons Why Python is So Popular

The main thing that most people will want to know when getting into this type of programming is why it is so popular. There are so many different programming languages out there. Each of them is created with a simple goal of communicating with computers better, but this is not always the result. Many of the programming languages out there are so challenging and complicated to use that it ends up frustrating a user and making them give up on their dream of being a computer program. The whole reasoning behind the Python Programming method was to provide an easy to use language for programmers to use in any application.

One of the biggest reasons for the popularity of Python is that it allows more to be done in a shorter amount of time. Because more can be done with fewer lines of Python code, it takes far less time to develop an application. For the computer programmer looking to churn out multiple applications in a day, Python is just the right fit. Most developers consider the use of Python as a no-brainer due to the amount of time it saves and the versatility that it has. Rather than toiling away for hours on end with Java or C++, you can do the same thing with Python in half of the time.

The next reason why Python is so popular is that it helps you to create code that is very easy to read. To work within a code and tweak, you will have to be able to read it quickly. The primary goal of Python Programming developers was to make their code the easiest to read out of all of the coding languages out there. Because this code is so easy to read, it will take you far less time to scan it and make the changes needed. When using coding languages like Java, you will spend hours going through each line of code. Even the smallest error in coding can make an application malfunction. Using Python allows you to find mistakes in a hurry and correct them before any problems occur.

Due to the simplicity of the Python coding system, the time it takes to learn it is significantly reduced. You will not have to worry about perfecting odd rules to have success with this coding language. Many people who have a bit of experience in coding will be able to start using Python right away. Being able to hit the ground running with this type of coding will allow you to get applications made in no time. If you are looking to start your programming career in a hurry, then the only logical choice you have is to learn Python.

The versatility that Python has is also a big selling point for most people. This coding language can be used in browser-based applications and XML. If you are into developing user interfaces or even interacting with other databases, you will be able to use Python to do so with ease. After you have perfected the art of Python Programming, you will be able to use it in any application development process. Having this versatility will allow you to take on a variety of jobs in some different industries.

Now that you know all about why people use computer code, you are ready to delve in deeper to the world of Python Programming. In the next chapter, you will learn how to get a copy of Python for your system and how to download it properly. By having your copy of Python, you will be able to work with it and figure out how to use it for your application development.

To create programs using this type of programming method, you will have to get an application to enter the code into. There is an alternative to getting an application like this, which is writing the application using what is called machine code. This process is a tough one and may lead to you becoming frustrated and giving up on this task altogether. The applications out there made for Python will allow you to type in the code and run it to see what it does in real time. This means that you will be able to find and address mistakes with ease when downloading these programs. In this chapter, you will be able to find out how to get these programs and how best to use them for your particular needs.

Understanding the Platform

Before you can start to use these programs, you will need to understand what a platform is. The short explanation of a platform is the combination of the computer's hardware with an operating system. A platform will have specialized rules that dictate how it will run. The details of how a platform runs will be hidden from you in the Python application. This means that as you type in the code, the Python application will turn it into something that can be used by the platform as a layout. Making this program work successfully will require you to find a Python version that works for the particular operating system that you are running.

Due to the overwhelming number of platforms out there, you will have to invest some time and effort into getting the right Python program. By going here, you will be able to get a list of different downloads. The main part of this page will have links for the most popular downloads like Mac, Windows or Linux. There is a list of links on the left of the screen that give you alternate Python settings to use if needed. If you are looking for a more updated editor than what comes in the regular download, you will be able to find it in these alternate settings. Regardless of what platform you are using, you will be able to find a Python program that works for it.

Installing the Python Program

Once you have found the download that will work for your platform, you will be ready to install it on your computer. Here is what you will need to do to install on the various operating systems out there.

Windows and other Similar Systems

If you are using the Windows or similar operating systems, you will need first to find the file that you have downloaded from the Python site. The name of the file will vary, but you can usually find it by searching the word Python in your folder search box. Once you have found this download, you will need to double click it to get started. Usually, a dialog box will pop and ask you if you are sure you want to run this file. You will click run to get the process started. After you click run, the wizard program will guide you through what you need to do to get the program going. This program will ask you where you want to put the files downloaded from the Python program. Creating a specific folder for this program and placing all of the records there is the best way to be able to keep up with them. You can do a custom install where you put the various files in different locations, but this takes a lot of time and is usually not necessary. Running the program on the Windows system will be easy when using the Command Prompt option. When opening Command Prompt, you will be able to type in Python to get the program to come up.

Using the Mac System

If you are a fan of all things Apple, then chances are you are using a Mac rather than a PC. Python has a version that is compatible with the Mac, which means you should have no problem getting it installed. Once you have downloaded the file, you will need to double-click it and start the process of getting it on your computer. When you initiate this download process, you will be asked to put in your administrator password. Once you see the Install Succeeded dialog box, you will be able to start using your new Python program.

In any programming language, variables and data types are two of the most important concepts you will come across. After all, variables form an integral part to all complex programs.

What are Variables?

Variables are simply memory locations that have been reserved for the storage of values. In other words, you will actually be reserving some space in the memory when you create a variable.

The interpreter will allocate memory to the variable based on its data type. It will also decide what can be stored in that specific reserved memory with the help of the data type. Therefore, you can store decimals, characters or integers in these variables by assigning the right data type to the variable.

Assigning Values to a Variable in Python

In Python, you do not need to explicitly declare a variable in order to reserve space in the memory unlike other programming languages. Instead, the declaration will take place automatically when a value has been assigned to a variable. In order to assign a value to the variable, the equal sign is used. The operand located to the left of the = operator will be the name of your variable. The operand located to the right of this operator will be the value that you wish to store in the variable.

The following example shows how you can assign values to different variables in Python.

#! /usr/bin/python

Counter = 100   # an integer assignment

Miles   = 1000.0   # A floating point

Name = "John"   # A string

Print counter

Print miles

Print name

As you can see in the above example, counter, name and miles are all variables while the values that they have been assigned are 100, John and 1000.0 respectively. On executing the code shown above, the following result will be produced.

100

1000.0

John

Assigning Multiple Variables in Python

There is no need to use multiple statements for assigning values to variables in Python. There are different ways by which this can be achieved.

You can certainly take a single value and get it assigned to multiple variables at the same time. In order to know how to accomplish this, take a look at the following example shown below.

a = b = c = 1

On the other hand, you can also assign different values to different variables at the same time. You simply need to make sure that each consecutive object has been separated by means of a comma. You can even assign different values of different data types simultaneously. The following example shows you can do this.

A, b, c = 1, 2, "john"

The Standard Datatypes in Python

The fact is that you can store data of different types in memory. Take the example of a person. The age of the person will be numeric but the name will be only alphabetic. On the other hand, the address of the person will consist of alphanumeric numbers. That is why Python offers a range of standard data types which can be used for defining the operations that are possible on them. The data types also determine the storage method available for the variable.

There are quite a few data types available in Python. Some of them are listed below.

- Numbers
- List
- String
- Tuple
- Dictionary

We will be taking a look at each of these data types in greater detail in turn. However, there is one little thing that you should know first.

Conversion of Datatypes in Python

There can be a number of situations in which you need to convert a particular variable from one data type to another. In order to perform a conversion between types, you simply have to use the name of the data type as a function. There are a number of built-in functions in Python which allow you to convert a variable from one data type to another. These functions will return a new object that represents the converted value. Take a look at the functions as shown below.

Int(x [, base])

This will convert x into an integer. Here, base specifies what the base will be if x happens to be a string.

Long(x [, base])

This will be converting x into a long integer. As with string, base states what the base will be when x is actually a string.

Float(x)

This will be converting x into a floating-point number.

Complex (real [, imag])

This will create a complex number

STR(x)

This will convert object x into its string representation.

repr(x)

This is going to convert object x into an expression string.

eval(str)

This will take the string and evaluate it and then return an object.

tuple(s)

This will convert s into a tuple.

List

It will be converting s into a list.

Set

This will be converting s into a set.

Dict (d)

This will create a dictionary. In this case, d has to be a sequence of tuples with key and values.

Frozenset

Here, s will be converted into a frozen set.

Chr(x)

This will convert an integer into a character. In this case, x is the integer.

Unichr(x)

Here, x has to be an integer. It will be converted into a Unicode character.

Ord(x)

This will be converting a single character into its integer value.

Hex(x)

Here, an integer will be converted into a hexadecimal string.

Oct(x)

This will be converting an integer into an octal string.

Now that data type conversions are over with, let us take a detailed look at the different data types available in Python.

Number Datatypes in Python

As the name suggests, number data types will be storing numeric values. This data type is immutable. In other words, if you change the value of a number data type object, and entirely new object will be allocated. You can easily create a number object by assigning a value to them.

The following example shows you how you can assign a number variable.

var1 = 1

var2 = 10

It is also possible to delete the reference to any number object by means of the Del statement. The syntax for this statement is given below.

Del var1 [, var2 [, var3 [...., varN]]]

The Del statement can also be used for deleting a single object or even multiple objects. The following example shows you can do it.

Del var

Del var_a, var_b

Kinds of Numerical Datatypes

Python offers support for four different kinds of numerical data types. They are as follows.

Int: These are called either integers or ints. They are signed integers and they can be either positive or negative. They are whole numbers and do not have any decimal point.

Long: These are long integers and they are often referred to as longs. These integers can be of unlimited size. They are written in the same way like integers but are followed by an L in the lowercase or the uppercase.

Float: They are floating point real values and are also called floats. These are representative of real numbers and they will be written with a decimal point that divides the integer and the fractional parts. Floats can also be written in scientific notation. E or e will be used to indicate the power of 10.

Complex: They are complex numbers and their form is "a + bJ". Here, a and b will be floats while J is representative of the square root of -1 which is, of course, an imaginary number. Complex numbers are rarely used while programming in Python.

Converting From One Number Type to Another

Python is capable of converting the numbers internally in expressions that contain mixed types to a common type for the sake of evaluation. However, there can be situations in which the number has to be explicitly converted from one number type to another. This is usually done so as to fulfill the requirements of a function parameter or an operator.

The statements that can be used for this purpose are given below.

☐ int(x)

This will convert x into a plain integer.

☐ long(x)

This will convert x into a long integer.

☐ float(x)

This will convert x into a floating-point number.

☐   complex(x)

This will convert x into a complex number. The real part will be x while the imaginary part will be zero.

☐   complex(x, y)

This will convert x and y into a complex number. The real part will be x while the imaginary part will be y. In this case, both x and y will be numeric expressions.

String Datatypes in Python

Of all the data types available in Python, strings are easily the most popular. They can be easily created by using quotes for enclosing a few characters. In Python, single quotes are given the same treatment as double quotes. In other words, they are the same. It is quite easy to create a string. All you need to do is assign a value to a variable. Take a look at the example given below.

var1 = 'Hello World!'

var2 = "Python Programming"

Accessing the Values in a String

The fact is that Python does not have a character data type. Instead, they are considered to be strings that have a length of one. As a result, they are also considered to be a substring. In order to access the substrings, you should be using the square brackets with the index so as to slice them and get the substring that you require.

The following example shows how you can access the value in any string.

#! /usr/bin/python

var1 = 'Hello World!'

var2 = "Python Programming"

Print "var1 [0]: "var1 [0]

Print "var2 [1:5]: "var2 [1:5]

After executing the code shown above, you will find the result to be the same as shown below.

var1 [0]: H

var2 [1:5]: ytho

Updating the Values in Strings

It is possible to update a string that already exists by re-assigning a variable to a different string. The new value that you get can be related to the previous value that you have or it can be a completely new and different string. Regard the following example to understand how strings can be updated.

#! /usr/bin/python

var1 = 'Hello World!'

Print "Updated String: - ", var1 [:6] + 'Python'

On executing the code shown in the above example, the following result can be derived.

Updated String: - Hello Python

String Formatting Operator in Python

The string format operator is % in Python and it happens to be one of the best features of this language. The operator is completely unique to strings. There are quite a few symbols that can be used with the % operator.

The following example shows how this operator can be used.

#! /usr/bin/python

Print "My name is %s and weight is %d kg!" % ('John', 21)

After executing the code show in the above example, the result that you will notice is given as follows.

My name is John and weight is 21 kg!

Use of Triple Quotes

The triple quotes available in Python serve a very useful purpose. With them, you can let your strings be written over multiple lines including TABs, newlines and other special characters. You should already be familiar with triple quotes as shown earlier in the book.

The following example illustrates the use of triple quotes.

```
#! /usr/bin/python

para_str = """this is a long string that is made up of

Several lines and non-printable characters such as

TAB (\t) and they will show up that way when displayed.

NEWLINEs within the string, whether explicitly given like

This within the brackets [\n], or just a NEWLINE within

The variable assignment will also show up.

"""

Print para_str
```

On executing the code shown above, the result produced is shown below.

This is a long string that is made up of

Several lines and non-printable characters such as

TAB (   ) and they will show up that way when displayed.

NEWLINEs within the string, whether explicitly given like

This within the brackets [

], or just a NEWLINE within

The variable assignment will also show up.

As you can see, all special characters have been converted to their printed equivalents without any errors. You should also remember that newlines can occur with an explicit carriage return present at the end of the line. Alternatively, the escape code of newlines (\n) can be used for this purpose.

Raw Strings

Raw strings will not consider the backslash to be a special character. Instead, all characters placed inside the raw string will remain the same without any change. Check out the following set of examples.

#! /usr/bin/python

Print 'C: \\nowhere'

As you can see, this is not a raw string. As a result, it will end up producing the result shown below.

C:\nowhere

The example given below, however, does make use of raw string. See how the r'expression' has been used.

#! /usr/bin/python

Print r'C:\\nowhere'

On executing the code shown above, the result produced is given below. As you will notice, the string has not undergone any change unlike the previous example.

C:\\nowhere

So far, we have learned about the number and the string data types in Python, what they are and how they can be used. There are three other data types that you should know about but we shall be tackling them in the next chapter.

The sequence is the most basic of all the data structures available in Python. In a sequence, each element will be assigned a number which denotes its index or its position. The first index will always be zero while the second index will be one and this way it will go on.

There are six types of sequences that have been built into Python. However, the most commonly used ones are lists and tuples. They are the ones you should know about at the moment. You will learn about the others as you progress into the more advanced stages of learning Python.

There are quite a few operations that can be done with all the sequence types. Those operations include slicing, indexing, adding and multiplying among others. Additionally, built-in functions are available in Python that allow you to find the larges and smallest elements in a sequence as well as its length.

Lists in Python

Lists are the most versatile of all the data types available in Python. It can be written as a sequence of values or items separated by means of commas and located between square brackets. One of the most important features of lists is that the items present in the list can be of varying data types.

The following example shows how you can create lists. As you will see, it is very easy to make a list.

list1 = ['physics', 'chemistry', 1997, 2000];

list2 = [1, 2, 3, 4, 5];

list3 = ["a", "b", "c", "d"]

Accessing the Values in a List

If you want to access the values present in a list, you need to use the square brackets to slice along with the indices so as to get the value present at that specific index. Take the following example into account.

#! /usr/bin/python

list1 = ['physics', 'chemistry', 1997, 2000];

list2 = [1, 2, 3, 4, 5, 6, 7];

Print "list1 [0]: "list1 [0]

Print "list2 [1:5]: "list2 [1:5]

After you execute the code shown above, the result that will be shown is given below.

list1 [0]: physics

list2 [1:5]: [2, 3, 4, and 5]

Updating a List in Python

It is possible to update single and even multiple items present in a list. You simply need to give the slice on the left side of the assignment operator. The following example shows how you can do so.

#! /usr/bin/python

List = ['physics', 'chemistry', 1997, 2000];

Print "Value available at index 2:"

Print list [2]

List [2] = 2001;

Print "New value available at index 2:"

Print list [2]

After executing the code shown above, the result that will be produced is shown below.

Value available at index 2:

1997

New value available at index 2:

2001

Deleting Elements in a List

It is possible to remove a single or even multiple elements from a list. However, the procedure depends on whether you know which element you wish to remove. If you do know the exact element that needs to be removed, the Del statement can be used. If you do not know, then the remove () method will have to be used.

The following example shows how the Del statement can be used.

#! /usr/bin/python

list1 = ['physics', 'chemistry', 1997, 2000];

Print list1

Del list1 [2];

Print "After deleting value at index 2:"

Print list1

On executing the code in the example shown above, the following result will be displayed.

['Physics', 'chemistry', 1997, 2000]

After deleting value at index 2:

['Physics', 'chemistry', 2000]

Tuples in Python

Like lists, tuples are also sequences of Python objects. However, the objects are immutable. As a result, it is not possible to change tuples unlike lists which can be changes whenever required. Moreover, a tuple will be using parentheses unlike lists which use square brackets. On the other hand, creating a tuple is similar to creating lists and the process is simple. You simply need to put the different values separated by a comma. Alternatively, the values separated by commas can be placed inside parentheses.

The following example illustrates how tuples can be created.

tup1 = ('physics', 'chemistry', 1997, 2000);

tup2 = (1, 2, 3, 4, 5);

tup3 = "a", "b", "c", "d";

It is also possible to create an empty tuple. You simply need to use the parentheses without placing anything inside. The following example illustrates the creation of an empty tuple.

tup1 = ();

In order to create a tuple that contains a single value only, a comma has to be included. Take a look at the following example.

tup1 = (50,);

Accessing the Values in Tuples

In order to access the values inside a tuple, you will have to use the indices for slicing them and obtain the value present at a specific index. Take a look at the example given below.

#! /usr/bin/python

tup1 = ('physics', 'chemistry', 1997, 2000);

tup2 = (1, 2, 3, 4, 5, 6, 7);

Print "tup1 [0]: "tup1 [0]

Print "tup2 [1:5]: "tup2 [1:5]

On executing the code given above, the following result will be produced.

tup1 [0]: physics

tup2 [1:5]: [2, 3, 4, and 5]

Updating Elements in Tuples

As tuples are immutable, it is not possible for you to update or modify the values of the elements present inside one. On the other hand, you can take parts of an existing tuple and then create a new tuple. The following example shows you how this can be achieved.

#! /usr/bin/python

tup1 = (12, 34.56);

tup2 = ('abc', 'xyz');

 # following action is not valid for tuples

 # tup1 [0] = 100;

 # So let's create a new tuple as follows

tup3 = tup1 + tup2;

Print tup3

The following result is produced when the code given above is executed.

(12, 34.56, 'abc', 'xyz')

Deleting Elements in Tuple

Again, it is not possible to remove individual or multiple elements in a tuple because of the immutable nature of tuples. On the other hand, you can create a new tuple by adding all the elements that you want from the previous tuple while skipping out the ones that you wanted to get rid of. This process is rather easy and you already know how you can extract specific elements out of a tuple.

Of course, you can easily remove an entire tuple if you want. To explicitly remove tuples, the Del statement can be used. The following example demonstrates this action.

#! /usr/bin/python

```
Tup = ('physics', 'chemistry', 1997, 2000);

Print tup

Del tup;

Print "After deleting tup:"

Print tup
```

The result produced on executing the code shown in the above example is given as follows. You will notice that an exception has been raised. This is due to the fact that the tuple tup does not exist anymore once the Del statement has been executed.

('Physics', 'chemistry', 1997, 2000)

After deleting tup:

Traceback (most recent call last):

  File "test.py", line 9, in <module>

    Print tup;

NameError: name 'tup' is not defined

Dictionaries in Tuple

The dictionary data type in Python can be said to be a hash table type. If you are familiar with Perl, you will notice that they tend to work like hashes or associative arrays. A dictionary is enclosed by means of curly braces while its elements can be assigned or accessed by means of square braces.

An element in a Python dictionary consists of a pair of key and value. Any data type in this programming language can be used for the dictionary key as long as they are immutable. Therefore, the data types used for the key are numbers, strings or tuples. On the other hand, values can be any arbitrary object in Python. Each key will be separated from its associated value with the help of a colon (:) while the elements are separated with the help of commas. In any dictionary, the keys in it will always be unique but the values may not be.

Accessing the Values in a Dictionary

The process to access the elements present in a dictionary is similar to what you have done for lists and strings. You need to use the square brackets. However, instead of indices, you will be using the key so as to obtain the value. The following example shows you how you can do so.

#! /usr/bin/python

Dict = {'Name': 'Zara', 'Age': 7, 'Class': 'First'}

Print "dict ['Name']: "dict ['Name']

Print "dict ['Age']: "dict ['Age']

On executing the code shown above, the following result will be produced.

Dict ['Name']: Zara

Dict ['Age']: 7

You must make sure that you are trying to access the element with the right key. If you try to use a key that is not a part of the dictionary an error will be shown. Take a look at the following example.

#! /usr/bin/python

Dict = {'Name': 'Zara', 'Age': 7, 'Class': 'First'}

Print "dict ['Alice']: "dict ['Alice']

Upon executing the code given above, you will find the following result has been produced.

Dict ['Alice']:

Traceback (most recent call last):

  File "test.py", line 4, in <module>

    Print "dict ['Alice']: "dict ['Alice'];

KeyError: 'Alice'

Updating the Dictionary

It is possible to update the dictionary easily. You can add a new pair of key and value. You can also change an existing entry or even delete an existing entry. The process is illustrated in the example shown below.

#! /usr/bin/python

Dict = {'Name': 'Zara', 'Age': 7, 'Class': 'First'}

Dict ['Age'] = 8; # update existing entry

Dict ['School'] = "DPS School"; # Add new entry

Print "dict ['Age']: "dict ['Age']

Print "dict ['School']: "dict ['School']

After executing the code shown in the above example, the following result will be produced.

Dict ['Age']: 8

Dict ['School']: DPS School

Deleting the Elements in a Dictionary

It is possible to remove individual elements in a dictionary in Python. Alternatively, you can get rid of all the elements present in the dictionary. Of course, the entire dictionary can be deleted and that too in a single operation. The Del statement can be used for explicitly removing the entire dictionary. The following example demonstrates how this will be possible.

#! /usr/bin/python

Dict = {'Name': 'Zara', 'Age': 7, 'Class': 'First'}

Del dict ['Name']; # remove entry with key 'Name'

dict.clear ();   # remove all entries in dict

Del dict;   # delete entire dictionary

Print "dict ['Age']: "dict ['Age']

Print "dict ['School']: "dict ['School']

The execution of the above code will cause the following results to be displayed. You will notice that an exception will be raised. This is because the dictionary dict does not exist once the Del statement has been executed.

Dict ['Age']:

Traceback (most recent call last):

  File "test.py", line 8, in <module>

    Print "dict ['Age']: "dict ['Age'];

TypeError: 'type' object is unsubscriptable

The Properties of the Dictionary Keys

The values present in a dictionary do not have any restrictions. You can use any arbitrary Python object. They can be user-defined objects or standard objects. On the other hand, the keys of the dictionaries need to follow some important rules. Those rules are given below.

Duplicate Keys Not Allowed: It is not possible to have more than one entry for each keyword. Therefore, there cannot be any duplicate keys in your dictionary. If duplicate keys are encountered during assignment, it will be the last assignment that gets the preference.

#! /usr/bin/python

Dict = {'Name': 'Zara', 'Age': 7, 'Name': 'Mani'}

Print "dict ['Name']: "dict ['Name']

On executing the code given in the above example, you will find the following result has been produced.

Dict ['Name']: Mani

Keys Must Always Be Immutable: You have to ensure that the keys chosen are of an immutable nature. Therefore, the data types that you can use as dictionary keys are numbers, tuples and strings. Check the following example to get a better understanding.

#! /usr/bin/python

Dict = {['Name']: 'Zara', 'Age': 7}

Print "dict ['Name']: "dict ['Name']

The following result is produced on executing the code given in the above example.

Traceback (most recent call last):

　File "test.py", line 3, in <module>

　　Dict = {['Name']: 'Zara', 'Age': 7};

TypeError: list objects are unhashable

Chapter 6
Enjoy the Ease of Ruby

Developed in the 90s, Ruby is one of the most recent programming languages in the world. Even so, it is remarkably popular thanks to its dynamic and open-source nature. It is an object-oriented programming language which was designed to possess an easily readable syntax that could be written even by a beginner. There is no need to learn and memorize a huge list of commands to get started with Ruby.

Ruby is known to be a programming language that is quite easy to learn. In fact, it is possible to pick up the basics in less than an hour. You can find a quick start guide that will take around 20 minutes to complete by the end of which you will be acquainted with the fundamentals of this programming language. If you are already familiar with Python, learning Ruby will become less of a challenge.

Another thing you need to keep in mind is the difference between Ruby on Rails and Ruby. You see, Ruby is a programming language. On the other hand, Ruby on Rails is a framework that has been built with Ruby. While Ruby is a general purpose scripting language, Ruby on Rails allows the development of web applications.

The Features of Ruby

There are some excellent features in Ruby that make it a useful programming language to learn. Here are some of the top features.

Flexibility: Although Ruby is an object-oriented programming language, it also provides support for imperative, functional and procedural programming. As a result, it is quite flexible for many programming requirements.

Objects: In Ruby, you will find that everything is considered to be an object. This also applies to numeric values. This greatly simplifies programming in this language.

Blocks: One of the best features of Ruby is the blocks. These are blocks of code which can be used as a parameter in a method. This greatly simplifies Ruby programming allowing you to build code libraries easily. These libraries can be used to provide various functionalities to code blocks that you build later.

Scalability: This is another excellent feature in Ruby. You can easily maintain programs written in this language even they are quite big.

A Simple Program in Ruby

As with other programming languages, here is the basic Hello World example program written in the Ruby language.

#! /usr/bin/ruby -w

puts "Hello, World!"

As you can see in the example, the program is incredibly simple with only a single line of actual code. This goes on to show how easy it is to learn and write programs in this language.

The Syntax in Ruby Programming

In any programming language, you need to pay attention to the syntax of the code. Improper syntax can cause errors during runtime or even break the program and give results that are different from what is expected. In Ruby, the syntax concepts are quite simple and easy to understand. Here is some of the syntax concepts that you need to know when programming in this language.

Whitespace

In Ruby, whitespace characters such as tabs and spaces are typically ignored by the program. However, they will be taken into account when they are present in strings. Be that as it may, there are certain cases in which white spaces are used for interpreting ambiguous statements. These interpretations can produce warnings if the −w option has been enabled.

Line Endings

In Ruby, newline characters and semicolons are treated as the ending of statements. However, if operators like backslash and + are placed at the end of a line, Ruby will treat them as an indicator that the statement is going to be continued.

Identifiers

Identifiers are the names given to methods, constants and variables. In Ruby, identifiers are always case sensitive. Therefore, 'Hi', 'HI' and 'hi' will be treated as different identifiers in Ruby. On the other hand, you can make use of alphanumeric characters as well as the underscore character in making your identifiers.

BEGIN and END Statements in Ruby

These are two important statements in Ruby. You are certain to come across situations where you need to use these statements as you program in this language.

The BEGIN Statement

This statement allows the code under it to be declared before the actual program is executed. Therefore, the code in the BEGIN statement will be the first to be executed. You can use multiple BEGIN statements, and they will be executed in the order they appear in the program. The basic syntax of this statement is given below.

BEGIN {

#code

}

The END Statement

This is the opposite of the BEGIN statement as the code it declares will be executed at the end of the program. The syntax for this statement is given below.

END {

#code

}

Variables in Ruby

There are four different kinds of variables in Ruby. Understanding them is vital to Ruby programming. Here is a short introduction to these variables.

Class Variables: As the name suggests, these variables belong to a specific class and are available to the different objects in that class. It is also a characteristic of that class. They will be shared among the descendants of the module or the class in which they were defined. You need to initialize them before you can use them in method definitions. If the -w option is usedthen; warnings will be produced when the class variable is overridden. All class variables have to start with @@.

Instance Variables: These variables will be available for different methods for a specific object or instance. Therefore, instance variables will be different for different objects. If uninitialized, the instance variable will have the value of nil and it will cause warnings if the -w option has been used. All instance variables will have to start to @.

Local Variables: The scope of these variables range from the start of a block of code to its end. In other words, it exists between the braces. They are not available outside the method. If you reference an uninitialized local variable, Ruby will consider it to be a call to a method which has no arguments. It is possible to declare local variables by assigning to uninitialized local variables. All local variables have to start with either an underscore or with a lowercase letter.

Global Variables: These variables are used when you need to have a variable that can exist for all classes. By assigning to global variables, you can change the global status. As such, their usage is not recommended unless absolutely necessary. They can complicate the program. Uninitialized global variables will have the value of nil. With the -w option, they can cause warnings.   All global variables need to start with the '$' character.

Conditional Structures in Ruby

There are quite a few conditional structures available in Ruby, most of which are common to other programming languages. Therefore, you should not have a problem if you are familiar with other languages. Even if you do not, it will not be difficult for you to learn.

• **If statement:** This statement is used to execute a block of code when a condition is determined to be true. The execution of the code will be skipped when the condition returns false.

- **Else statement:** The else statement is used with the if statement. It provides an alternate block of code to be executed when the condition is evaluated false.

- **Elsif statement:** The elsif statement is used with the if and else statements and is put between the two. It is possible to add as many elsif statements as required. This statement is used when you need multiple conditions to be checked. The elsif statement which returns true for the condition will have its block of code executed.

- **Unless statement:** The unless statement is the opposite of the if statement. It used when you want a block of code to be executed when the condition returns false.

- **Case when statement:** Using the if-elsif-else conditional structure can get quite complicated when you need to evaluate a lot of options. In these situations, you can apply the case when statement. The code under the when statement will be executed when the condition returns the right value. Multiple when statements can be applied to a case statement. It is also possible to use the else statement with this conditional structure. The else statement will give a block of code to be executed when the condition does not return any value acceptable to the when statements.

Loop Statements in Ruby

Loops are also available in Ruby. As you already know, loops allow you to execute a certain block of code several times. Here is a short introduction on the loops available in Ruby.

•   **While loop:** The while loop allows the code to be executed as long as the condition is true. Once it turns false, the execution is stopped, and the program heads over to the next statement.

•   **Until loop:** This is the reverse of the while loop. The until loop will keep being executed as long as the condition is false. It will stop when the condition becomes true.

•   **For loop:** While Ruby offers a for loop, it is not similar to the for loops available in other programming languages. Instead, the for loop in Ruby functions more like the for each loop in other programming languages. As a result, it will execute the code as long as there are elements to consider in a given expression.

You should be now familiar with the basics of programming in Ruby. Of course, there are still a lot left to go, but these details should help you prepare for the difficult parts.

Conclusion

With the end of this book on programming languages, I hope that it has proven to be useful for you. You should now know about the easiest programming languages for beginners to start with.

Of course, the introduction to programming should have familiarized you with the fundamentals of the activity in general. After all, there are quite a few things that are similar to all languages. One of them is that all languages require you to adopt the mentality of a programmer. Once you do so, you will find programming relatively easier.

As you will have noticed in the book, five languages have been chosen: C, Java, JavaScript, Python and Ruby. These were chosen not only because they are easy to learn but also because they introduce you to the world of programming in a way few other languages can. They are versatile, and you will find it easier to learn other more advanced programming languages.

You should now be familiar with the features of each of the programming languages and know how to write the basic Hello World program for each. You will have also learned some of the basics for all of these languages.

I wish you all the best for your future in programming. With a bit of perseverance and hard work, you will find yourself writing complex code in no time.

Before you jump on your computer, I would like you to post an HONEST REVIEW on Amazon.com in order to improve the quality of the book.

Thank you.

Made in the USA
Middletown, DE
23 December 2016